Too Much the Sun

A Play

Nicholas Pierpan

A Samuel French Acting Edition

SAMUEL
FRENCH
FOUNDED 1830

SAMUELFRENCH-LONDON.CO.UK
SAMUELFRENCH.COM

FOR AMATEUR PRODUCTION ENQUIRIES

UNITED KINGDOM AND WORLD
EXCLUDING NORTH AMERICA
plays@SamuelFrench-London.co.uk
020 7255 4302/01

Each title is subject to availability from Samuel French,

depending upon country of performance.

TOO MUCH THE SUN

First performed at the Moser Theatre, Wadham College, Oxford, on 25th February 2003 with the following cast of characters:

Man	Beau Hopkins
The Soros	Thomas Eastcott
Sergeant Goodarm	Ross Burley
Lestaines	Fergus Eckersley

Directed by Tom Farthing

CHARACTERS

Man, young man; around twenty-one years old
The Soros, older man; fifty plus years old
Sergeant Goodarm, an old seaman; sixty plus years old
Lestaines, foreigner, accent slightly strained. wears black; thirty plus years old

The action takes place in a coastal village in England

AUTHOR'S NOTE

An elaborate set is not required. One production had only a black box upstage and a large clock downstage. A couple of chairs were also used.

In this production all four characters occupied the stage for the entire performance. During and between the various scenes, they moved about the space in ways suggesting the interior movements of a timepiece: a character absent from a scene might be upstage, moving in a slow arc across the background; or between scenes the characters might spin into new positions. All the movements were simple, closely tied to the text and created physical relations between the characters that enhanced the tensions of the story. This approach solved several logistical problems and offered a number of imaginative possibilities. Some of these directions are already in the text but are kept to a minimum.

A NOTE ON THE TEXT

A slant (/) is used to note a moment of interruption between lines of overlapping dialogue.

FIREARMS NOTICE

With regards to the rules and regulations of firearms and other weapons used in theatre productions, we recommend that you read the Entertainment Information Sheet No. 20 (Health and Safety Executive).

This information sheet is one of a series produced in consultation with the Joint Advisory Committee for Broadcasting and the Performing Arts. It gives guidance on the management of weapons that are part of a production, including firearms, replicas and deactivated weapons.

This sheet may be downloaded from: www.hse.gov.uk. Alternatively, you can contact HSE Books, P O Box 1999, Sudbury, Suffolk, CO10 2WA Tel: 01787 881165 Fax: 01787 313995.

TOO MUCH THE SUN

SCENE 1

Somewhere on the stage is a clock, and somewhere else a black box

A Man sits in a chair, DC. *His look is of still concentration*

A Sammy Davis Jr song begins playing faintly, then grows in volume. Red lights come on, bathing The Man in red. The Man has a fit, writhing all over the chair. It's an epileptic seizure. Then he is still. The red lights go down. The music fades

Silence

Man Don't worry. Happens all the time. Sometimes it's worse. Especially when you're all alone. Having other people around is a big help. But nothing is worse than when you're in a queue at Sainsbury's, getting all ready to buy your Hob Nobs and tea, and then it hits. Everyone freaks out at once. You'd think they were the ones who got the seizures. And there's always some old biddies around, over seventy and so authorities on everything, and they always start screaming, "It's an epileptic! It's an epileptic! (My daughter's friend plays cards with an epileptic)." And that's fuel on the fire, of course. Someone else reckons I might be choking on my own tongue, because they've seen on the telly that that's what epileptics do, and so right away their hands are all in my mouth. And when I come to — in the middle of pure bedlam — I'm thinking, "Next time, I'll just stay at home and stick needles in my eyes. It's cheaper and less painful."

Of course, medication makes it all a lot easier. But it's not like the doctors actually know what they're talking about. This thing I've got, it has its own order to it — its own method to the madness. Case in point: before a seizure comes on, I always hear Sammy Davis Jr. More than that, I can see him. I can see him singing. I was never a fan, you know? It just happens. Then things go red. And I know I'm in for it. You should see the look on a doctor's face when you ask him to explain Sammy Davis Jr. Who can? He was black and he was Jewish, you know what I mean?

The doctors, they can't explain why Sammy's looking for me, or why it's always him. The worst is when I'm driving in a car, all alone. If I hear Sammy, it's time to pull over. He's coming for me. If you have a seizure while you're driving? Well, fill in the blank. Something people never think about. For an epileptic, driving is a very serious issue. It's a very complicated thing. You've got to avoid the roads in the early morning and at dusk, because when the sun is near the horizon, its light comes for you through the trees — flickering through leaves and branches. Like some kind of strobe. That's some very dangerous shit. Very dangerous stuff, the sun. And it's a totally natural phenomenon, you know? You have a fit, you lose your driver's licence for two years. Minimum. But I love cars like anyone else! I love driving on sunny days. The oncoming calm of evening … I mean, these bureaucrats — they're denying me my humanity!

And so I'm stuck in this bed-sit by the pier. Watching nothing happen. When it's not *my* fault Sammy comes looking for me. From out there.

His mobile phone emits a text-message sound. He doesn't seem to notice

Sammy always comes from "out there". He's waiting to sneak up on me, the way invisible messages invade a phone. And then announce themselves.

He looks at his mobile phone and reads the message

This is what I've been waiting for. Somebody important wants
to talk to me: The Soros himself! Out on his estate. (*He smiles,
genuinely*) Class.

A doorway opens US

Goodarm is standing in the doorway looking outside

There is the sound of rain

*The Man remains sitting in the same place and facing forward
throughout the scene*

Goodarm Oh dear. It's starting to come down now. You made
it just in time! But there's no one here.

Silence

The Soros is out. He won't be able to make it into harbour in
this. Why don't you come back tomorrow?
Man I can't.
Goodarm Eh?
Man I can't leave. The rain. When the streetlights come on and
flash through the falling rain, it can trigger my seizures ——
Goodarm I'm sorry. I forgot. Sorry.

Silence

How's the family?
Man They're still dead.
Goodarm Right. Sorry about that. I forgot ... Sorry.
Man Can I stay until it stops?
Goodarm Would you like me to close the door?
Man No. I like the sound of rain.
Goodarm It is a nice sound. Quite *harmless* really ... but, you
know — I never understood why it had to rain in the harbour.
I know the land needs rain, for flowers and things ... But the

sea, well, you know there's enough water there already. And when the sea gets rough, and you're out in the thick of it trying to save some fisherman who's adrift in the waves, or rescuing someone who's misread the tides and gotten stranded on the causeway, well ... Thunder and rain just makes it all worse now, doesn't it? Funny how storms only happen when the seas are rough.

Man How long were you the coxswain of that lifeboat?

Goodarm Before I got into the security business?

Man Yeah.

Goodarm Royal National coxswain, twelve years.

Man (*incredulously/sarcastic: mocking the fact that someone so daft would have such an important job for so long*) Jesus Christ.

Goodarm doesn't notice the sarcasm

Goodarm That was a good job. The way we *did* things. Our lifeboat was always at sea within five to eight minutes of a call-out. If I was fishing and they needed me, they would launch and pick me up on the way. And the sea! It was always a ... battle. But I learned, from the day I started to the day I stopped. You can't think about the sea, you can't even look at most of it, most of it's underwater! But you learn from it — how terrible it must be to suddenly find yourself adrift in thirty-foot waves as hard as concrete, and not know if anyone's coming for you. A boat once sank forty miles off the coast with two men on board — their lifeboat had gone down with the rest of it — and we found them clinging to a gas cylinder. The skipper, we couldn't get him to let go, we had to pry his hands off that cylinder. He'd lost himself. You know ... I haven't thought of that day in ages. The Royal National retired me, and I haven't even got memories of it left over. I forget things. Those memories, they're in me *somewhere* but I don't find them until I'm reminded. Usually, there's just this.

Long silence

Man (*laughingly, as if to cheer Goodarm up*) What about your "security business"?

Goodarm What about it?

Goodarm disappears. On the opposite side of the stage The Soros appears

The Man and The Soros begin speaking as if in the middle of a conversation

Soros I tell you, he's trying to kill me!

Man That's ridiculous.

Soros He's trying to kill his own employer! It's unnatural!

Man I realize you're upset/ but surely ⸺

Soros Upset? The man is stalking me. I hired him as a security guard, to protect me from *out there* when I'm *in here*, and the man is trying to murder me ⸺ I have proof.

Man Proof?

Soros Well, *evidence*.

Man Like what?

Soros Like ... intent. Intent to kill me.

Man He's an old man who tells stories. Harmless. So harmless I never understood why you hired him.

Soros Pity! That's why!

Man But do you really think being a security guard suited him?

Soros Of course not, look what's happened. I've armed him and now he's coming for me.

Man Doubtful.

Soros It's true ⸺ I tell you Sergeant Goodarm is living on my grounds, he's protecting my grounds ⸺ he'll get away with it.

Man If you're so scared, get rid of him. He's got a pension.

Soros And stoke his murderous fires of rage?

Man You're mad. The "pillar of the community" has gone insane. The Soros/ has gone ⸺

Soros The Soros is the only one clever enough to see the source of his own demise.

Man An old man who tells stories.

Soros The Soros is the only one clever enough to see the source of his own demise. And it's killing him.

The Soros disappears. Goodarm appears

We return to the scene between Goodarm and The Man, as if in mid-sentence

Goodarm When the weather was bad, really bad, all kinds of stormy rain and thunder, we would have to dock that lifeboat and sit in the shelter on the beach, just waiting for emergency call-outs to come in. On days like that, we knew the calls would come. Dangerous business. Everyone would be tense, watching the telly or staring at the walls. I'd just sit myself down by the *open doorway* and try to make friends with the weather, sit there on the dry steps in front of the *rain-door*. That's what I called it on days like that. I knew we would be heading for a close shave out on the sea, but when I stared at that rain-door … I'd lose myself in the storm as well. And the message it brought would make me think I was an Indian, an American Indian like you see on the telly … I wasn't myself, but I didn't mind it. I'd see myself in face paint and a gown of feathers — then we'd get a call and I'd sit in the cox real upright, feeling savage and purposeful. Brave.

And it was sad. I remember a little lad, not past ten, we found washed out in the tides. Drowned. He must have been playing in the water and drifted off. I didn't say anything, but everyone in the lifeboat knew I was the one who would carry this little boy off the boat when we finally docked, that he would be in my arms — and when I did it … it felt like a sacrifice. But the rain-door never told me why the storms only come when the seas are rough. I just always thought, somehow, Nature would know better. It usually does … *provides* for us. But sometimes, Nature makes you play the fool. I don't like that. And I don't like it here, working for men like The Soros, with all their money and *inventions*.

Goodarm disappears. The Soros appears

We return to the scene between The Soros and The Man, as if in mid-sentence

Soros I need your help, that's what I'm saying.
Man Because I'm a thief?
Soros *Thief* is a strong word.
Man But the name sticks.
Soros Of course it does, you're a *car thief* for Christ's sake ...

Silence. The Soros recovers himself

> I thought you had decided to go away, get a fresh start after you got out. I supported the idea. I sent you money. Why did you come back to the village? Have you come back to clear your name? Is that it?

Man No.
Soros Well why not — why shouldn't you want to clear your name?
Man Because I did it. Because they caught me red-handed. Everyone knows that.
Soros But you *knew* whose car it was. Why did you do it?
Man Because I was tired of walking in the cold. The rain was starting to come down. I saw its dry leather seats, its steering wheel promising to take me wherever I wanted to go. Its clutch calling, asking me to test it. Purring. Like it was making me an offer. So I took it. The punishment came later.
Soros What was it like, inside ... not too bad I hope.
Man Thanks for all the money.
Soros Well I've got a job for you now, employment! That murderous rogue Sergeant Goodarm. He's after me. He's supposed to be protecting my grounds! And he's coming in here at night — I can hear him. I want you to find out why. This isn't in the contract!
Man You want a spy.
Soros Don't tell me he's a *friend* of yours.

Man I did know him. He would come to the workshop sometimes, outside of fishing season, and talk to my father. Hand
him things, tools. He knew about tools. But mostly he would
just stand there. Talk.

Soros To your father? The locksmith?

Man Yes.

Soros I see.

Man It might be clever to put in some new alarms.

Soros The house is listed.

Man Then maybe you should bring someone else in, to catch
him.

Soros That's why I need you. You're the one I'm looking for!

Man Me?

Soros Watch him. But keep your distance, avoid him if necessary. Keep an eye on him — on what he's up to. I'll pay you.
I'll pay you very well.

Man But what exactly is he doing?

Soros He knows this house. Knows his way around.

Man He tells stories.

Soros Like a bird of prey.

The Soros exits

*The Man begins walking clockwise around the stage, continuously,
as if he were descending a circular stairwell*

Man My first "job" since getting out of prison. "Watching Sergeant Goodarm." Sounds like a porn flick for peeping toms.
But it also sounds like some easy dosh. Clearly, The Soros
has gone insane again. It happens periodically. Ever since his
"great success." That is the man who invented the world's
first perpetual-motion machine. A little clock that never stops
ticking. He has the patents and everything. You don't even
wind it up. It just … goes … perfectly … Changed the way
the world keeps time. Made him very wealthy. Tick Tick Tick.
Amazing how quickly we all forget what he was like before.
I'm suddenly reminded. An obscure clockmaker in his tiny

shop. He was crazy then, too. Now that I remember … Like when he walked up Castle Hill and refused to come down. He went stark raving mad up there. No one could help him. Not many people cared. Three days and three nights. Then a Vicar from Holystone arrived. I thought there would be some kind of exorcism. But the Vicar saw how The Soros was dying from exposure, and simply instructed us to bury the corpse on Castle Hill. But to bury it standing upright, beneath a mound. With one hand held outward, an act of defiance to the sea. The same sea that had brought the murderous Vikings to destroy our village. This madman was sacrificing himself. In a holy act. To protect us from the sea. From what the sea brought.

Goodarm enters and walks counter-clockwise, as if he is ascending the same spiral staircase. He carries a toolbox

The Soros overheard all of this, and was suddenly cured. What a miracle. So the Vicar spent the rest of the day up on Castle Hill, admiring the seabirds, and smiling. But not friendly. More like he was about to tell the punchline to a funny story. But refused to at the last moment, you know?

The Man and Goodarm run into each other

What are you doing here?
Goodarm Oh! Ummmm … seeing the boss.
Man His ferry made it into harbour. You took his coat. He's fine. It's three in the morning.
Goodarm Well then. Time for a security check.
Man With tools.

Silence

Goodarm Your father used to visit this house a great deal, before it was sold …
Man Yes.
Goodarm Before he passed away, he would come in here on the weekends, to look at these locks. In the house. On the doors.

No one notices them. But they're incredible, unmistakable. Important. Quite intricate these locks, if you notice them ... each lock is different here ... in this old house. Your father used to tell me all about them, what he learned from them. Your father was a locksmith.

Man I know.

Goodarm So now *I* look at them. I learn from them, too.

Man You pick them — you unlock them.

Goodarm Yes.

Man Why?

Goodarm Because The Soros is the only one with the keys.

Man Maybe for good reason.

Goodarm I don't like him.

Man Why not?

Pause

What exactly you looking for, mate?

Silence. The Man cautiously moves past Goodarm, as if to continue his descent of the staircase and never mind the whole encounter

Goodarm You don't want to be leaving yet. The weather is still quite rough. There's a night fog out there and you'll lose yourself on the road.

Man I don't drive anymore. But thanks.

The Man again tries to get past Goodarm, as if to leave. Goodarm blocks his progress. The Man steps backwards uneasily

Goodarm Some nights, I'm out on those grounds, keeping everything "safe", but when the night fog comes in off the sea, I can't see two feet ahead of me — I can't see the stones on my path until I'm upon them, and sometimes ... when the fog clears ... I suddenly realize I'm not where I thought I was. I'm somewhere else. Maybe I find that I'm just outside my bungalow, and can pop inside for a cheeky cup of tea. But maybe I'm gone out, past the barns, through every field, and when the fog lifts I find myself between the tall trees — who look down on me, like I'm an ... *invader* or something. Their stillness ... well you know it's like ... an accusation ... When the fog comes back down there's just *me* again, looking to find my way home. That's when I start having real problems ... hearing things ... Haven't you heard of how the night fog used to make the old forty-gun ships lose their way? The fog would lift and they'd discover that they'd sailed into an enemy fleet by mistake! It happened to Lord Nelson! Once, when the fog lifted, he suddenly found himself in between two columns of Spanish warships. He could see their tall masts. That's not where he wanted to be! He'd lost his co-ordinates. It was all an accident. A mistake. That Spanish fleet immediately collapsed on Nelson's ship, firing cannons upon it from both sides. But that's when the night fog returned ... just in time ... Nelson was able to slip through the Spanish lines undetected and escape. Like a ghost. Leaving those blind columns of the Spanish fleet to fire upon each other ... to sink their own men.

Darkness

The Man and Goodarm exit

The Lights come up on The Soros. There is a large sack sitting near his feet

Silence

Soros I've always hated ghost stories. Dreaded them. You think you'll grow up and if some satanic hobgoblin actually does invade your house, live in your cellar, or hide under your bed, you'll be able to combat it, kill it, protect your family from it. The same way you imagined as a boy that your father would come to protect you, if you needed him. And maybe now, you find yourself an old man with no family, although still bright

and daring in the daytime, running your own highly success-
ful business, a bold entrepreneur in the region, but at night the
stories come back to you.

Pause

Like "The Fur Collar." Two girls at home alone, their parents
gone out for the evening. There is a heavy storm. The electricity
is cut. So the young girls play games in the darkness — one
puts on her mother's coat, the one with the gorgeous fur collar, and walks around the large house. The other tries to scare
her by popping out of a closet, or jumping up from behind the
sofa. They collapse in laughing hysterics. Later, they turn on
the radio. There's a murderer on the loose. Now the fear is
real. They hear a window shatter downstairs. One of the girls
goes to investigate — still wearing the mother's fur coat. Her
sister remains in the bedroom. Locks the door. Silence. And
finally a knock at the bedroom door. Totally quiet. Then another
gentle knock. The girl in the bedroom opens the door but can
see nothing in the darkness — she reaches out her hand and
feels the fur collar of the coat, and then the stump where her
sister's head used to be.

The electricity may be cut, but that radio still broadcasts dis-
turbing news. This time to me. I have reason to fear.

*The Man enters, wearing a black leather jacket and a black
cap. He startles The Soros*

Man (*with a cockney accent*) Evenin' guvnor.
Soros I told you to stop calling me that.
Man I thought you liked it. I thought it was a nice touch.
Soros It's obscene. Take off that ridiculous hat! As if Goodarm
    wasn't bad enough — my so-called surveillance expert has a
    fetish for leather!
Man I don't want him to see me.
Soros Take it off.
Man I don't want to be noticed. I need the black.

Soros Part of the problem. I'll have no Hell's Angels in this house, as if Goodarm wasn't bad enough — has he gone to sleep yet?

Man He's here. Inside.

Soros Again?

Man He picks the locks, goes where he wants. He's steady.

Soros And you left that lunatic alone? Are you mad?

Man I haven't a key for every door — he loses me.

Soros Is there anyone with him?

Man Begging your pardon but I was wondering / if you could ...

Soros I said is there anyone with him?

Pause

Man Just him. But he's steady.

The Soros takes out a chain of keys and gives them to The Man

Soros Take care of those. Follow Goodarm, wherever he goes. Do your job.

The Man goes to leave, examining the keys on his way out. He pauses

Man This place suits you.

Soros It certainly does. Because it's mine — isn't that wonderful? And I intend to enjoy it. Remember what happened to poor Miss Bates all those years ago — murdered by a lunatic on her own estate — terrible business. We don't want that. People still talk about it.

Man I know, but they always say ... it was a ghost that got her.

Pause

Soros It wasn't a ghost. It was a lunatic.

Man It was neither. My father and I worked for her, we'd drive all the way up there to clean the locks on her windows and doors. And she wasn't *murdered*, by a lunatic or anyone else. It was just that, in the winter, she rowed herself out to sea ...

and she didn't row back. No one knows why. She was the last of her clan, no husband, no children ... living in that great big house all alone: twenty-five bedrooms and no heir. And then that was it. The police asked my father to come and unlock the house for them. No one owned it anymore.

Silence

Soros (*in near panic*) You mean there was no lunatic?
Man She was crazy. And alone. That's enough. Her body was never found. The house was left empty. After my father opened it, that is.

The Man goes to exit

Don't wait up.

The Man exits

Soros opens the sack and takes out a gun. He then takes out a clock and a screwdriver, and begins tinkering with the clock

The Lights go out on The Soros. He remains seated in the same position in the darkness

Goodarm appears elsewhere, carrying a toolbox

The Lights come up on Goodarm

Goodarm There was a house once. Not like now. I lived there when I was youngest. There the fairies hid behind living-room plants, animals called me from ocean-corners, the trees pushed ladders up their own trunks, so that I could go and read in sight of the sea. On daring days I would walk down its rocky coast and sit in the company of waves, as they coupled with the salt rocks — and when I leaned farther into them, I soon found myself quite well-read. But it was always cold. Even when the water would finally feel warm, when I came out again onto the rocks I was freezing.

The Man appears, carrying the keys

Man It's like he wants to be caught. Wandering around here every night. The Soros tells me to hang back a little longer. One more night, he says. Monotony. (*He looks at the keys, the way they jingle*) These keys. My father. Growing up in that workshop, big lock-cutter in the corner — with all of its sharp turns so painfully scripted by my father — I hated him. His epilepsy. Because he gave it to me. Because of the way it drove him in his work. The way that poor man spent all his time perfecting the interiors of all those precious locks. Like he was trying to cure himself, his own mind. But after I'd been caught stealing cars. On the inside. I was so thankful for the epilepsy. That it killed my father before I got pinched. He never had to visit me in prison. My father the locksmith. The Soros a little clockmaker. Once upon a time they started a silly club in the village for "local craftsmen." Not only were they the club's founders, but also its only members. (Typical for these parts.) My father and The Soros would hold meetings in the old smugglers' caves, out on the Islands. An excuse to drink. But they always said a third craftsman was needed to make the fellowship perfect. Because, you see, *precision metalwork* comes from locks, clocks, and guns. All three share the same technology, on the inside, the same metalwork, which is very beautiful I suppose, but ... Aren't guns what you need, if you're going to drink in a smugglers' cave?

The lighting intensifies. It illuminates The Soros as well, who has remained in the same position. He is now holding the gun, as if ready to fire. In his lap is an open clock and a screwdriver — as if he has been taking the clock apart. They are not directly aware of each other's presence

Goodarm I wonder how we are able to live in this world without freezing.
Man In smugglers' caves, of all places.
Goodarm Look how the world resists us.

Man Not that they had much choice.

Goodarm It still covers itself with water. It still covers itself with ice.

Man At low tide, there are twenty-eight islands. But at high tide, only fifteen are left.

Goodarm I think that is why the fishermen believe that when they die, their souls are transferred to seals.

Man Most of them are naked rocks. Uninhabitable.

Goodarm Yet when seals overpopulate the islands — and become a danger — we cull them. Norwegian hunters come to do the necessary and remove the carcasses.

Man I wonder what it's like on those small islands: after every fissure has been cracked by the dry sun, to then be smashed and covered by the sea. Eggs of the seabirds utterly drowned.

Goodarm You might feel slightly chilly if you drew your own conclusions.

Man A man chained himself to a small island. He wanted to spend a night there and look beneath the tides. With lots of oxygen tanks, he looked like some kind of astronaut.

Goodarm How are we able to live in this world without freezing?

Soros Prometheus.

Man A lifeboat rescued him in the end.

Goodarm This place is bleak and barren and lacks the sun.

Soros Not the property of that rock, or that bird.

Man And no complaints were issued by the coxswain.

Soros Or anyone else.

Goodarm Still we have no image of Nature. We carry no image of Man.

Man I actually envy that kind of daring.

A long silence

Soros My house has become silent for a reason. The clock cases of my antique timepieces are now empty. It is a large collection. I have dismantled my precious clocks. Quietly detaching the screws and pins, I have removed the interiors of each antique timepiece. A *security* issue. The shells, the cases, are left behind. Looking as if they had never been touched. Even the dust on them undisturbed. Like the work of a skilled thief.

Silence

Man That's what scares me. Catching Sergeant Goodarm is going to put me out of a job, and they don't come easily anymore. I'm more than just a convict. My father was a locksmith. Unflattering irony that isn't lost on the local crowd.
Goodarm At low tide, twenty-eight islands. At high tide, fifteen are left.
Man My father loved those smugglers' caves.

Sammy Davis Jr's "Bye Bye Blackbird" begins to play

There is an expressionistic dance sequence between actors to the music

   Lestaines enters and takes the black box

The Man has a seizure

Black-out

SCENE 2

An empty stage

The Man lies on the floor DS *. He looks as if he's just woken up, but time has clearly elapsed since the last scene. He's surrounded by empty, hollow clocks on the floor around him. He looks very bored*

Man I wake up in the afternoon, in my little bedsit, and I do nothing ... for a long time. Maybe I go out for a bite to eat. I run into people, or they run into me, and they say "hi" to me, like we're old friends. I don't know who they are, but I pretend I do, you know? They don't know the difference, so there's no harm done. They must have known my father. But there's nothing really to be done in the village, and I start wondering what I'm doing there. All the friends I grew up with have moved far away. Of course ... I think about following them ... Then I walk out here, not long after dusk, hop over the fence, and find Goodarm ... but he's not a danger. He's just a mumbling idiot. When I ran into him that first night — it was like he didn't remember me. He knew my face, but when I looked at him ... Nothing registered. And The Soros ... He comes home from visiting his clock factories and doesn't do much. I reckon he spends all his time here either watching *University Challenge* on the telly, or masturbating. Or generally just storming about and winding himself up ... sending me text messages ... Usually it's about how Goodarm's trying to kill him. "This is the night!" He says, "*Hard evidence* is what I'm looking for, keep your eyes open!" He also likes muesli. With yogurt. Thinks it's sophisticated or something, but I reckon he's just trying to be Swiss. Some nights I see Sammy Davis Jr. Then I wake up and ... things seem different for a while ... Different from when I wake up in the afternoon. That's really about it.

My father liked it here. But I never came with him. He'd ask me to come along, tell me how they'd collected locks from all over the world on the doors of this old house ... but after helping him in the workshop all week — I hardly wanted more of it on the weekend. If I could do it again, I would have come with him. Spent more time with him. A shite job this is, but ... it makes me feel like I'm a kid again ... that I'm walking around with my father. That I took him up on all those offers. Like I'm making up for lost time. That's all over now. Nothing left. But it keeps me in the village. And so here I am.

Lestaines enters, carrying the black box, behind The Man

Black-out

The Man and Lestaines exit

The Lights come up

The Soros is alone, gun still in hand

Soros The greatest clock of them all sinks beneath the horizon. I have created its rival. Perpetual clocks that changed the world. Always ticking. Always precise. The original? Kept safe in its black box. A masterpiece of invention. Allowing me to stand with Da Vinci, and Di Giorgio; they knew the majesty of a machine. Artists of mills and gears — not fishes and butterflies! And Da Vinci dreamt of hanging clocks, that could drive their own weight, ticking forever. An image of eternity. *Harmony* of verge escapements, pendulums, chains and weights. Hours, minutes, seconds ... Dials showing lengths of days; aspects, age, and phases of the moon; an astrolabe showing the sun's progress through the zodiac; schedules of the tide; calendar disks for Saint's days, the dates of Easter for a century ... A machine to mirror the universe — with loud bells coordinating people into tightly interlocking patterns. I perfected the interior of this machine! A non-stop clock. Keeps up with the universe. A great invention. Appearing to me in a little black box. Purely functional at the time — mirroring nothing! Simple. But as valuable as fire. Prometheus.

Silence

I must destroy the boy.

Goodarm enters

Goodarm I'm sorry I'm late.
Soros Ah! You're here! At last!
Goodarm I'm sorry I'm late.
Soros Very late.

Goodarm How late?

Soros How should I know? All my clocks are gone. Only the
clock-cases are left. And you still haven't caught him!

Goodarm Maybe it's not the boy.

Soros It's what thieves do! It's what he's done.

Goodarm I only caught him once. Before things started to
disappear. He had empty hands.

Soros Did you call the police?

Goodarm No.

Soros Did you warn him?

Goodarm Yes.

Soros And what did he say?

Goodarm That he was here to visit you.

Soros And you believed that?

Goodarm I made him some tea.

Silence

Soros I suddenly realize you may not be suited for this job.
He's comes in here at night stealing my things. Defacing my
clocks. And my security guard just *wanders around* like some
muttering idiot.

Goodarm I have seen him on the grounds many times. From a
distance. Like a ghost.

Soros So catch him! That's why I hired you! I thought you
were *just* the man for the job. For catching *him*. For putting
him away!

Goodarm Why's that?

Soros Because he stole your car. He demolished it for fun.

Pause

Goodarm Yes. I had forgotten. That was some time ago.

Soros And people died.

Goodarm is unresponsive

The lifeboat was short of men. You were retired, fitting ships into bottles down in your cellar. They rang you. And you didn't make it to the harbour in time because you suddenly realized your car had been nicked.

Goodarm Yes. I remember.

Soros They had to leave without you.

Goodarm Everyone died.

Soros You were still at home. Looking for your car.

Goodarm They were short of men.

Soros You could have saved them.

Goodarm The ones they had gone to rescue.

Soros Some were children.

Goodarm Yes. I remember.

Soros Do you see where all this is going?

Goodarm No.

Soros I've armed you — it's in your contract — the man is a trespassing psychopath — he's hollowing out my clocks — isn't the message obvious? Why do you hesitate? People died! Shoot that boy! His thefts are casualties.

Pause

Goodarm But he saved my life. I remember that storm. Every broken wave. I watched it roar from the harbour. I was soaked and blistered by the wind. A gale blowing in the heavy rain. And I saw that lifeboat when it finally drifted ashore. Emptied. They were all going to die. When a storm like that turns ugly, there's not much you can do.

Silence

Soros You're fired.

Silence

Goodarm exits

There is more to a clockmaker than the metalwork of time.

He examines the gun in his hand

The first were simple blacksmiths ... but when locks, clocks, and guns arrived — all at once — there came to be men like Jacques Yoleas: "a clockmaker and a gunner." "A reputed expert in matters of bombards." But those were the days. You couldn't rein those men in. Soon they were everywhere! Wide-ranging inventors —locks —clocks — guns — moving from one field of craftsmanship to the next, the most dynamic group in society! Later, we specialized ... We were lost ... Back in my "smaller" life, I started a club in the village to revive some of those lost ideals. I gave it a go with the boy's father. The "lock/clock" jokes between us were endless. And we drank a lot. He was a nice enough man. But not *noble*. He had no noble ambitions. It was so hard to get him out of his locks. That way of thinking. He was obsessed. His mind ... wasn't right ... But I was quickly becoming clockmaker-cum-gunfounder. And learning from him about locks, broadening my horizons ... An all-rounder. Like Prometheus — who inherited not only the secrets of fire, but also the secrets of metalwork ... in *all* its ancient forms ... But then, one day, in the smugglers' caves, I was opening two tins and in walked "Lestaines." That was his name. I called him the Black Prince. It was the only colour I ever saw him wear. And he just appeared right in front of us, like some kind of conqueror.

Elsewhere on stage, Lestaines and The Man appear, facing each other

The Man is standing, as if at a recital. Lestaines holds the black box. The Soros is not aware of them throughout, and vice versa

Lestaines Tell me the story again. Tell me the story correctly this time.

Man With little land to feed them, the men of those islands began looking for the big fish. And they all wore heavy sweaters. Patterns woven into them, a different pattern for each family. Because some of them would die at sea, where fish feed on the faces of the dead. But when a faceless corpse was found, the sweater remained to identify his clan.

Pause

That is why he gave his son such a sweater, when that boy left for the sailing ships. But his son died in a faraway ocean ... eyes eaten out, face moulted ... When his body was found, no one knew what the sweater meant.

Silence

Will you let me go?
Lestaines Tell me a story.
Soros Lestaines, in his black clothes — he said he was a gunsmith from over the sea, and wanted to join our fellowship (which was evidently becoming rather renowned). But as soon as we received Lestaines, our group broke into two camps. Him and the boy's father were both obsessed, going on and on about guns and locks ... self-protection ... they ignored my clocks, my ideals! There was a period when timekeepers were welcomed everywhere: a well-kept clock in the town was the sign of a well-run community ... But for Lestaines, all of this was just some Gordian knot to be blasted through as elegantly as possible. With one of his black walnut guns, I suppose. They had the same ethos, him and the locksmith: "Protecting what is yours" — madness. This fellowship was not about what was owned. As co-chairman of the fellowship, I expelled Lestaines. It was the only rational thing to do. And when he left, there was a serious falling out among the club's founders. It is not uncommon. But still, the locksmith and I saw each other on occasion. Talked. Then his son went to jail — fatherless — and the world moved on. But soon Lestaines was back.

Lestaines Tell me a story.

Man Of all the shipbuilders, he was the most cursed. They all suffered losses ... but he had been disinherited by the sea. It rejected each of his vessels, broke them on the rocks ... He was losing himself ... That was why he built such a strong boat for his son — to prove to the others that his hands were not blighted by the gods. Now that father walks the beach all day long ... waiting for his son to return, inventing errands to explain the boy's absence ... becoming himself a wandering pariah ...

Soros The day of my great success — when all the cameras came to this little town and I was officially proclaimed to be "a modern Prometheus". Lestaines found me. Amid that entire, glorious circus, he pulled me aside when no one was looking — and that's when I realized he'd found a new obsession ... Because that's when he whispered in my ear that it was not Prometheus who brought fire to the earth. Carefully, measuredly, he explained the importance of getting my stories straight. All of Africa, Asia, and the Eskimos knew it was thieving Raven who brought fire to the earth — who stole the lightning from the belly of a whale. Why was he telling me all of this, and on such an important day? How Raven had just been drying his clothes on a beach, when a whale came swimming quite close to shore. Raven called out: "Next time you come up for air, open your mouth and shut your eyes." Then Raven slipped quickly into his clothes, pulled on his Raven mask, and flew out over the water. The whale came up. She did as she'd been told. Raven darted through the open jaws and straight into her gullet. The shocked whale snapped and sounded. Raven stood inside and looked around.

Black-out on The Soros

The Soros exits

Lestaines Tell me a story.
Man Knock-Knock.

Lestaines Stop embellishing, for Christ's sake.

Man Growing up in that workshop, big lock-cutter in the corner
— with all of its sharp turns so painfully scripted by my father
— I hated him. His epilepsy. Because he gave it to me. Because
of the way it drove him in his work. The way that poor man
spent all his time perfecting the interiors of all those precious
locks. Like he was trying to cure himself, his own mind.

Lestaines Yes.

*Lestaines gives The Man the black box. The Man inspects it with
brief curiosity, they nod at each other*

The Man exits with the black box

Silence

Then the oracles commanded that the very next person to ar-
rive at the Temple be made King. Strange prophecy. Illogical.
A Phrygian peasant arrived in his car and was called to the
throne.

*The Soros enters. He stands near Lestaines but is not aware
of him*

Soros *No! Stolen! Stolen! My black box! Gone! How could I be
so stupid! How could I possibly …*

*The Soros freezes. He starts to laugh and is soon quite jubilant. He
stands up straight. From beneath his clothes, he pulls out a large
key that is hung around his neck, grabs it securely and relaxes.
He takes out a mobile phone, dials and presses to his ear*

*The Soros walks towards off stage with the mobile phone at his
ear*

Soros (*into the phone*) Hallo? Police?

Soros exits. The stage is empty

The Man enters, still carrying the black box Lestaines gave him

Man I wanted it. So I took it. It's as simple as that. It purred, after all. Made me an offer. So I took it. Then I slipped into the garage, cracked open the door of the Rover, popped the ignition and was on my way. Good riddance. The Soros was not what you'd call an "optimal" employer anyway. A tedious job with no future. Fuck him. And what a feeling! I hadn't done this in ages! You forget how much you enjoy something. *Now* I felt out of prison. And now ... (*Suddenly mystified*) I had this fucking box. What was I thinking? I don't know. But I had it. And the car. The Soros would come after me. So would the police. I tried opening the box while driving. Locked tight. This was something important I'd stolen. Brilliant. So I just drove faster. I didn't really care where I was going. I certainly wasn't going back. Back there. Back to prison. I should never have gone back to that village in the first place. Time to get away. (If you're aiming for a clean slate — I suggest you do so with a Range Rover. It really is the dog's bollocks.) I had the radio on and hit the gas. The road in front of me became more and more clear as the sun came up. I focused on the road, and not the breaking sunlight. But that was a silly idea. Because the sun was coming for me. Fully above the horizon now and fracturing its glare through the woodlands. I reached over to turn off the radio — I had to concentrate! But the radio was already off. It had never been on to begin with.

A Sammy Davis Jr song begins playing faintly, then grows in volume

It was Sammy I'd been hearing. Not now Sammy!

Sound of engine revving, then stopping

I pulled over. I pulled completely off the road and stopped the car.

Sammy Davis song fades to nil, replaced by singing birds. Gentle lighting. Silence

And I just sat there, in a lame Rover. Waiting to get caught. Was I mad? I was in a stolen car! For all I knew, I was carrying half the jewellery in Britain in this fucking box! But if you were me, you'd have sat there as well. And stared at the sun. Filtering itself through the trees. A bright light ticking through every leaf. It was all over me. Made my eyes hurt, but it also seemed quite harmless while I was sitting there ... wrapped in its blankets ...

Silence. The Man grows more claustrophobic, despondent

Where the hell was I? Not too far from the village. Those bastards would catch me. And I couldn't do anything about it now, except wait. I held the black box, and picked at its lock. It was never going to open. From the look of it, I was going to need a small bomb ...

Silence

Fuck it.

Sound of engine revving, pulling out onto road. The Lighting turns more red. Sammy Davis Jr song begins playing, louder and louder

Fuck prison. Fuck the whole thing. It was just light coming through the trees!

There is the sound of car screeching and crashing as the stage turns bright red

The Man has a seizure and collapses with box in hand. A car horn is heard. Black-out. The car horn continues as the lighting fades to gentle morning light. The car horn fades. Birds sing. The box is open. The Man wakes

That's when I saw it. The box, it was open. The lock had been triggered somehow, the lock had been triggered quite cleanly … Inside — completely full of this — machine ... Dials and levers, springs and cogs, a fucking mess. All of it moving at once. This was one of The Soros's famous clocks; there was no mistaking the resemblance. What was he doing, building one in a box? And it was just the naked machine, no clockface to hide parts of it. All so sharp and precise! Its gears were spinning razors. They hollowed the back of my eyes! As dials revolved in the chaos. Without numbers. Transfixing ... The box snapped shut. But I knew what to do. With a couple of pins and a wrench to hold open the lock, I stuck into its heart, manoeuvring my pick this way and that. All very precise, coordinated … but all very … irregular. A highly irregular sequence. Mimicking a crooked key, reeling awkwardly in every direction, to the shifting demands of this lock. But it was easy for me to follow. Because it was the jagged timing of my own mind. I stopped worrying about the police. And simply opened the box. Stared inside with wide eyes. Because this wasn't a *box* at all, or even a clock, this was a case. It shut itself again. The exhibition was over. I left it closed. Because I understood everything now. All at once. I'd seen it. Stamped in elegant letters upon the whirling bolts. "Stafford-Humnicus." My family name.

Darkness

The Man exits with the black box

Goodarm and Lestaines enter. Goodarm stands packing a suitcase and Lestaines sits. Goodarm and Lestaines never acknowledge each other, but seem to be familiar with each other nonetheless

Goodarm They sent The Soros to jail for that. You just can't go around stealing things. That black box was never opened again. No one knew how. No one knew how the boy got it open to make the accusations he did. He had very little to work with. He couldn't even open it himself, although he tried many times.

He said he'd done it before, and when Sammy Davis Jr came back, he'd do it again. But Sammy Davis Jr is dead. Luckily, it didn't matter. There was enough circumstantial evidence to convict The Soros of theft, if not murder. They knew The Soros had stolen that black box from the boy's father. It was the clocks. Just by looking at them a little closer, people could tell where their designs had come from. From a lock. A very sophisticated lock. Implied by the constantly moving keyhole of that black box. Its perpetual motion corrupted into time-pieces. Its technology stolen, for the uses of that clockmaker. The lock remains impenetrable, constantly shifting. But people knew the truth, just by looking at what they had. And that's how it works.

Goodarm goes about his business. He pauses

That's how it works.

Lestaines A son is usurped from the throne. The counterfeit king offers him a series of challenges to regain his lost place. Impossible labours, for the sake of public relations. But the boy passes them all. So the king offers him a final obstacle, in front of an entire court of witnesses. Two envelopes for the boy to choose from. In one of them is written the word "King" and in the other is the word, "Death." A very fair way of settling controversy — or so everyone thought. But the boy is not a fool. He knows the king has written the word "Death" into both envelopes. That this is no choice, but a very public assassination. So the boy selects an envelope and sets it on fire. Torches it in front of the court witnesses, in front of the king. The boy brings the ashes to the king and declares, "This is my choice." Then he opens the other envelope, which reads "Death." You see, he made something out of nothing. That's how it's done. At its best. And that was the end of the king.

The End

FURNITURE AND PROPERTY LIST

Scene 1

On stage: Clock
Black box
Chair

Off stage: Toolbox (**Goodarm**)
A large sack containing a gun; a clock; a screwdriver (**The Soros**)

Personal: **Man**: mobile phone
Soros: chain of keys, large key on necklace, mobile phone

Scene 2

On stage: Empty hollow clocks

Off stage: Black box (**Lestaines**)
Suitcase (**Goodarm**)

LIGHTING PLOT

To open: general interior

Cue 10   To open Scene 2   (Page 17)
           General interior lighting

Cue 11   **Lestaines** enters, carrying the black box   (Page 18)
           Black-out

Cue 12   **Lestaines** and **The Soros** exit   (Page 19)
           Lights come up

Cue 13   **Soros**: " ... inside and looked around."   (Page 24)
           Black-out on **The Soros**

Cue 14   **Man**: "... and stopped the car"   (Page 26)
           Gentle lighting

Cue 15   **Man**: " Fuck it."   (Page 27)
           The lighting turns more red

Cue 16   **Man**: " ... coming through the trees!"   (Page27)
           Bright red wash

Cue 17   **The Man** has a seizure and collapses. Car horn (Page 27)
           Black-out. When ready lights fade to gentle morning

Cue 18   **Man**: "My family name."   (Page 28)
           Darkness. When ready bring up general interior
              lighting

EFFECTS PLOT

Cue 10   **The Man**: "... coming through the trees!"   (Page 27)
           There is the sound of car screeching and crashing

Cue 11   **The Man** has a seizure and collapses   (Page 27)
           Car horn fades slowly with lights

Lightning Source UK Ltd.
Milton Keynes UK
UKHW021913050320
359851UK00011B/791